Looking at Countries

THE USA

Kathleen Pohl

FRANKLIN WATTS
LONDON•SYDNEY

First published in 2009
by Franklin Watts

Franklin Watts
338 Euston Road
London NW1 3BH

Franklin Watts Australia
Level 17/207 Kent Street
Sydney, NSW 2000

First published in 2009 by Gareth Stevens Publishing
1 Reader's Digest Road
Pleasantville
NY 10570-7000 USA

Dewey number: 917.3
ISBN: 978 0 7496 8251 4

Senior Managing Editor: Lisa M. Herrington
Senior Editor: Barbara Bakowski
Creative Director: Lisa Donovan
Designer: Tammy West
Photo Researcher: Charlene Pinckney
Reading consultant: Susan Nations, M.Ed.

Photo credits: (t=top, b=bottom, l=left, r=right, c=centre)
Cover (main) © Bill Ross/Corbis; cover (inset) Shutterstock; title page © image100/Corbis; p. 4
Shutterstock; p. 6 Robert Glusic/Getty Images; p. 7t Sylvain Grandadam/Getty Images; p. 7b © Michael T.
Sedam/Corbis; p. 8 Shutterstock (2); p. 9 Harald Sund/Getty Images; p. 10l Steve Bly/Getty Images; p. 10r
Shutterstock; p. 11t Shutterstock; p. 11b Matt Campbell/Getty Images; p. 12 Will & Deni McIntyre/Corbis; p.
13t Bob Sacha/Corbis; p. 13b Paul Barton/Corbis; pp. 14 Shutterstock; p. 15t © Andre Jenny/Alamy; p. 15b
Shutterstock; p. 16 © Rudy Sulgan/Corbis; pp. 17–181 Shutterstock (3); p. 18r © Natalie
Tepper/Arcaid/Corbis; pp. 19–20 Shutterstock (4); p. 21t Paul Burns/Getty Images; p. 21b Janis
Christie/Getty Images; p. 22 Getty Images (2); pp. 23–27t Shutterstock (7); p. 27b © Brian Hamilton/Alamy.
Every attempt has been made to clear copyright. Should there be any inadvertent omission please apply
to the publisher for rectification.

Printed in China

Franklin Watts is a division of Hachette Children's Books,
an Hachette Livre UK company.
www.hachettelivre.co.uk

Contents

Where is the USA?

The United States of America, or USA, is part of North America. It borders Canada to the north and Mexico and the Gulf of Mexico to the south. It has long coastlines on two oceans – the Atlantic Ocean to the east and the Pacific Ocean to the west.

Did you know?

The USA is the third-largest country in the world in total area. Only Russia and Canada are larger.

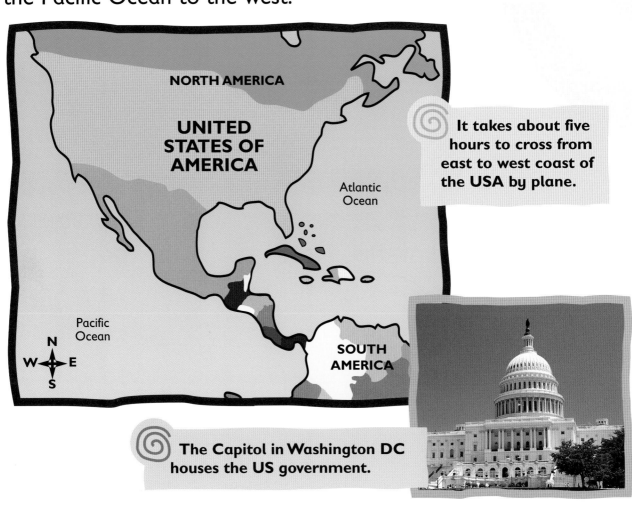

NORTH AMERICA

UNITED STATES OF AMERICA

Atlantic Ocean

Pacific Ocean

SOUTH AMERICA

N
W — E
S

It takes about five hours to cross from east to west coast of the USA by plane.

The Capitol in Washington DC houses the US government.

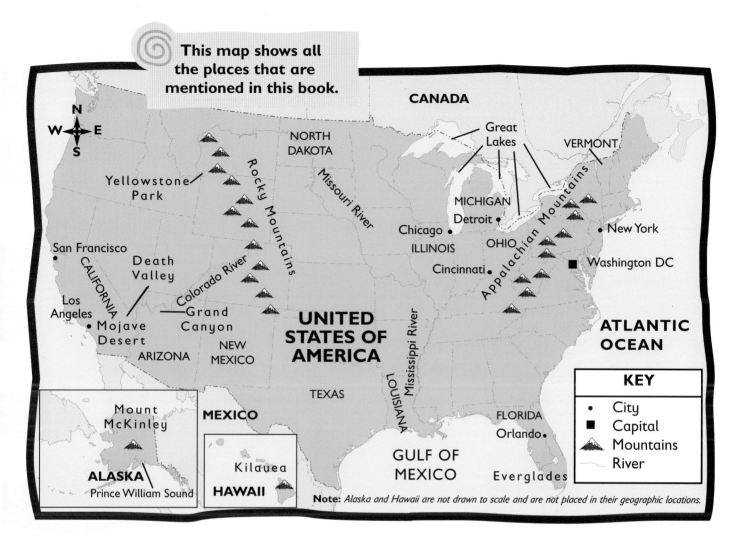

This map shows all the places that are mentioned in this book.

The USA is divided up into 50 states. They all follow the laws of the USA, but they also have state laws. Two of them, Alaska and Hawaii, do not share borders with other states. Alaska lies far to the north and shares a border with Canada. Hawaii is a group of islands in the Pacific Ocean.

Washington DC is the capital of the USA. The DC stands for District of Columbia. Government buildings and landmarks line its wide streets. It is home to the US president, who lives in the White House.

The landscape

The USA is a huge country and it has a vast range of landscapes. Beautiful beaches line the east and west coasts. High mountains and deep valleys cross the land. The Appalachian Mountains rise in the east while in the west the Rocky Mountains stretch from Alaska to New Mexico.

Wide plains and rich farmland make up the centre of the country. The Missouri River, the longest US river, flows across the plains. The Mississippi is the second-longest river and crosses the middle of the country.

Did you know?

The Grand Canyon is a wonder of the world. Over the course of millions of years, the Colorado River has cut through rock to form the canyon, or valley.

The Grand Canyon is about 1.6 kilometres deep. The Colorado River flows through the canyon in Arizona.

A swamp area called the Everglades covers a lot of southern Florida. Many animals, including crocodiles, alligators and huge turtles, live there.

Kilauea is a volcano on the island of Hawaii. It has been erupting since 1983.

Hot, dry deserts make up most of the south-west. Death Valley, in the Mojave Desert of California, is the lowest and hottest place in the USA. Mount McKinley, in Alaska, is the highest peak.

The islands of Hawaii were formed by volcanoes that built up from the ocean floor. A few volcanoes are still active, and sometimes blast smoke and ash into the air.

Weather and seasons

The bright colours of autumn leaves bring beauty to the north-eastern USA.

Most of the USA has four seasons – winter, spring, summer and autumn. However, the climate varies from region to region. The south-west is dry and desert-like. Hawaii and Florida have warm, wet, tropical climates.

Along the coasts, summer means fun in the sun for visitors.

In general, the northern states of the country are colder than the southern states. In parts of Alaska, snow stays on the ground for many months. Thousands of glaciers fill Alaska's mountain valleys.

Hurricanes sometimes form on the Atlantic coast and on the Gulf of Mexico.

On the Pacific coast, earthquakes can cause damage to people and buildings, especially in the area of San Francisco.

The Columbia Glacier in Prince William Sound is one of about 100,000 glaciers in Alaska.

Did you know?

The USA has the largest number of tornadoes in the world. These strong, swirling winds often damage land and buildings.

American people

More than 300 million people live in the USA. Native peoples lived on the land thousands of years ago. Later, settlers from Europe came to set up colonies. The settlers brought slaves from Africa. Today, the people of the USA have a mix of backgrounds.

Did you know?

The USA does not have an official language. Most people speak English. The second most common language is Spanish.

New York City is home to more than eight million people from many different backgrounds.

This Navajo girl from Arizona belongs to the second-largest Native American group.

The Statue of Liberty stands in New York Harbor. It is a famous landmark in the USA.

Chinese New Year parades are a popular custom in Chinese areas of the USA.

People from many countries have come to live in the USA. They are called immigrants and they often choose to live and shop in a certain area of a city. Some of them speak their native languages and continue to enjoy the foods and customs of the countries they have left behind.

Most Americans practise a religion. Many of them are Protestant or Roman Catholic. Other people are Jewish, Mormon, Buddhist or Muslim. A small number of Americans follow other religions.

School and family

Children must go to school until they are 16 years old. Many students go to state schools, others go to private or religious schools. A few children are taught at home.

About half of all children go to nursery or pre-school. At the age of five or six, most start kindergarten. Then they go on to elementary school, middle school and high school. They study reading, writing, maths, history and other subjects. Many students go on to university.

Did you know?

In 2008, almost 56 million students were in elementary school, middle school or high school in the USA. That is one out of every six Americans!

About three out of every four elementary, middle and high schools in the USA are state schools.

On farms and ranches, family members share daily chores.

Many American families celebrate holidays, such as Thanksgiving, by sharing a special meal.

The average number of children in an American family is two. Some children live with just one parent or other relative. Other children have two parents. In many families, the parents work outside the home. On holidays and birthdays, grandparents, aunts, uncles and cousins often celebrate together.

Country

At one time, most Americans lived in the country. They worked on small family farms or ranches. Today, only about two people in ten live in rural areas. Some farms are now owned by big companies. They have huge herds of animals on vast areas of land. Most farmers use modern farm machines.

US farmers sell their crops for money. In the Midwest, farmers grow wheat, corn and soya beans. They raise dairy cattle and pigs, too.

About nine million dairy cows live on US farms.

North Dakota is one of the top wheat-growing states.

Did you know?

People call the USA the 'bread basket of the world'. It gained that nickname because American farmers grow so much food.

Texas and some western states have large cattle ranches. In the southern states, farmers produce cotton, peanuts and tobacco. Pineapple, sugar cane, and coffee grow on plantations, or huge farms, in Hawaii. Farmers in Florida and California grow oranges and other fruits.

Rich volcanic soil and year-round sunshine make Hawaii a good place to grow pineapples.

City

In the past 50 years, many people have moved from the countryside to cities. Today, eight out of ten Americans live in or near cities.

New York City is the biggest city in the USA. It is home to more than eight million people. The streets are filled with traffic jams and the sound of honking horns. Tall blocks of flats and office buildings rise beside theatres, museums, shops and markets. Some people live in the suburbs – areas of housing near a city.

Did you know?

The tallest building in the USA is the Sears Tower in Chicago. The Empire State Building is the second-tallest skyscraper. It is in New York City.

The East River reflects the lights of the Brooklyn Bridge and the famous New York City skyline.

Los Angeles, California, is the second-biggest US city. It is home to Hollywood, the centre of the US film business. A huge 'Hollywood' sign stands on a hillside above the city.

Chicago, Illinois, is the third-largest city in the USA. Trucks and trains carry more goods in and out of Chicago than any other US city. Its airport is one of the busiest in the world. Elevated trains called the El run on tracks above streets.

In Chicago, elevated trains carry thousands of passengers each day.

Homes

Most new houses are built of wood or brick. In warm areas of the country, a lot of gardens have swimming pools.

Many people in big cities rent flats in tall buildings. Some cities have local housing styles. San Francisco, California, has streets of colourfully painted terraced houses.

Did you know?

About two out of every three people in the USA own their homes.

A colourful terrace of homes line this street in San Francisco.

Many blocks of flats have fire escapes on the outside of the building.

In rural areas, some people live in farmhouses. This wooden home is in Vermont.

This style is typical of many homes in the south-west.

Adobe, or sun-dried mud houses are common in the south-west. In rural areas, more people live in ranch houses or in big farmhouses. Some people even live in mobile homes, which can be moved from place to place.

Not everyone is wealthy in the USA. The cities have areas where poorer people live in run-down houses and blocks of flats. Some rural areas, such as parts of Appalachia in the east, have run-down homes, too.

Food

People in the USA eat many different kinds of foods. Favourites often vary by region. Fried chicken is a southern speciality. Spicy tacos and burritos are popular in the south-west. On the coasts, people enjoy fresh fish and seafood.

Louisiana's Cajun cooking is spicy and includes a lot of seafood. A favourite dish is a thick soup called gumbo.

In the north-east, a New England clambake includes lobsters, clams and corn-on-the-cob.

In coastal New England, lobster is a tasty but messy meal. Restaurants supply a bib, even for adults!

Pizza restaurants in Chicago, Illinois, are famous for deep-dish pies.

In big supermarkets, shoppers can buy all the foods they need.

Hot dogs are an all-American favourite.

In most cities, restaurants serve the foods of many different cultures. Fast-food restaurants are popular, too. Hamburgers, hot dogs, French fries and milk shakes are on the menu.

Thanksgiving is closely tied to food. Each November, Americans celebrate the holiday with a traditional roast turkey meal. The trimmings include stuffing, cranberry sauce and sweet potatoes.

Did you know?

Many people hold barbeques on the fourth of July (see p. 25). Americans eat about 150 million hot dogs on that holiday!

At work

Most Americans have service jobs. Some people are teachers, doctors or nurses. Others work in shops, banks and offices.

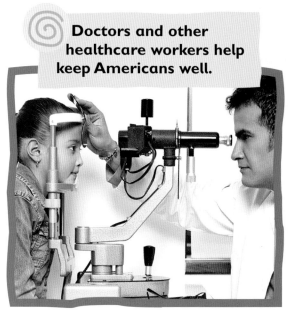

Doctors and other healthcare workers help keep Americans well.

Many office workers use computers on the job.

Did you know?

The USA buys more goods than it sells to other countries. Oil is the main import (product brought into the country).

This chef is one of the nine million Americans who work in restaurants or other food services.

Some people have jobs in tourism. They work in hotels, restaurants, airlines or national parks.

People who work in factories make many different types of goods. These include cars, aeroplanes and computers.

Detroit, Michigan, is called 'the Motor City'. Almost one million workers have jobs in the car industry there.

The USA has many natural resources. One natural resource is good farmland. The USA also has huge hardwood forests. People cut down the trees for wood to build houses and make paper. Some workers mine coal, iron ore, copper and gold. Others drill for oil.

Having fun

Many people in the USA enjoy sport. Baseball is so popular that it is called the national pastime. Americans watch major-league games at baseball fields and on TV. Many people play baseball and softball in youth leagues.

In the winter, American football fans watch the Super Bowl. Basketball, football, hockey, golf, swimming and other sports are popular, too.

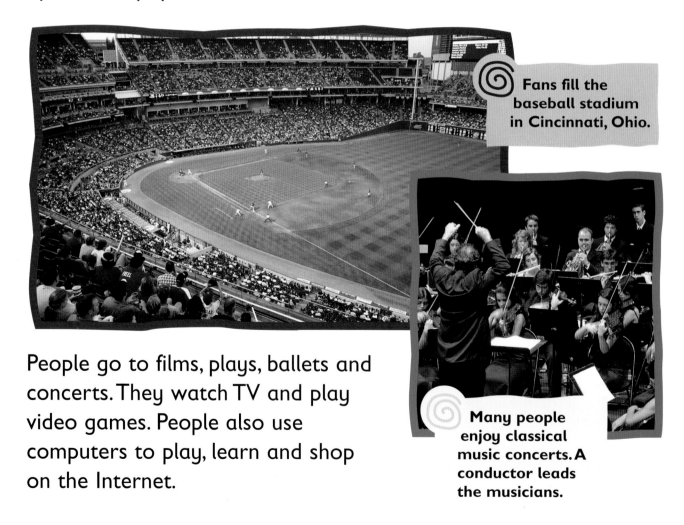

Fans fill the baseball stadium in Cincinnati, Ohio.

Many people enjoy classical music concerts. A conductor leads the musicians.

People go to films, plays, ballets and concerts. They watch TV and play video games. People also use computers to play, learn and shop on the Internet.

Yellowstone Park attracts holiday-makers who enjoy amazing scenery and good walks.

Americans like to take holidays. They visit all sorts of parks – national parks, theme parks and water parks. Some travellers enjoy skiing or camping trips.

Thanksgiving is a special American holiday. On that day, people give thanks for their blessings. Independence Day is celebrated on the fourth of July. On this day Americans celebrate their country's freedom from Great Britain with parades, picnics and fireworks.

Did you know?

Orlando, Florida, is the most popular summer holiday spot in the USA. Its warm weather and fun theme parks attract visitors year round.

The USA: the facts

- In the 1400s and 1500s, Native Americans lived on the land that is now the USA. Over the next 200 years, people from European countries came to North and South America.

- British colonists settled along the eastern coast of North America. They lived under British rule for many years.

- The USA stated its freedom from British rule on 4 July, 1776.

- The USA is a federal republic. Its laws are based on a plan of government called the Constitution.

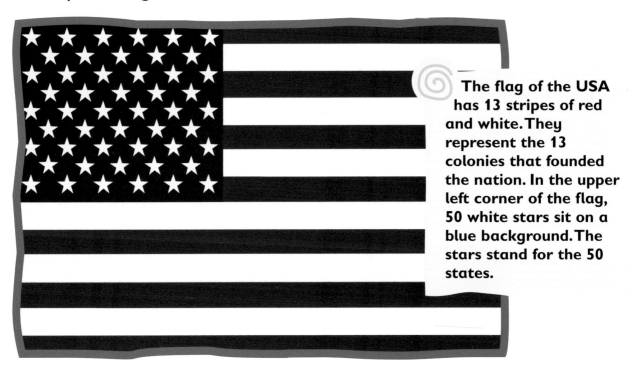

The flag of the USA has 13 stripes of red and white. They represent the 13 colonies that founded the nation. In the upper left corner of the flag, 50 white stars sit on a blue background. The stars stand for the 50 states.

• The USA is a democracy. The American people have a voice in their government. Citizens who are at least 18 years old can vote to choose their leaders.

• The president is the head of the government. George Washington was the first president of the USA. He served as president from 1789 to 1797. Washington is known as the 'Father of His Country'.

Did you know?

The bald eagle is the symbol of the USA. It stands for strength and freedom.

The bald eagle was named the official national bird in 1789.

The US unit of money is the dollar.

Glossary

adobe brick made of sun-dried earth and straw.

Cajun having come from French-speaking people who emigrated to Louisiana from a part of Canada.

canyon a narrow valley with steep sides.

colonies settlements of people who leave their native countries and go to live in other lands.

democracy government by the people, directly or through elected representatives.

factories buildings where goods are made.

federal republic a system in which the national government and the states have separate powers. Elected officials represent the people.

glaciers large masses of ice that move slowly over the land.

hurricanes storms with strong winds and heavy rains.

immigrants people who move to a country to live and work.

iron ore a mineral that contains iron and that is mined from the ground.

landmarks buildings or places of historical importance.

native born in a particular place.

natural resources elements in nature, such as oil and wood, that are used by people for industry.

New England the part of the north-eastern USA that includes Maine, New Hampshire, Vermont, Massachusetts, Rhode Island and Connecticut.

plains large areas of flat or rolling treeless land.

plantations very large farms on which a single crop is grown.

rural having to do with the country, country people or country life.

tornado a violent windstorm that looks like a funnel-shaped cloud.

tourism businesses that serve people who wish to travel to places for holidays or day trips.

tropical having a hot, wet climate.

Find out more

www.americaslibrary.gov/cgi-bin/page.cgi/es
Explore the 50 states of the USA.

www.whitehouse.gov/kids
The White House, home to the US president, has a special website aimed at children.

www.georgewashington.si.edu/kids/portrait.html
Examine a famous painting of former US President, George Washington.

Note to parents and teachers: Every effort has been made by the Publishers to ensure that these websites are suitable for children, that they are of the highest educational value, and that they contain no inappropriate or offensive material. However, because of the nature of the Internet, it is impossible to guarantee that the contents of these sites will not be altered. We strongly advise that Internet access is supervised by a responsible adult.

Some American words

Most people in the USA speak and write English, although many also know Spanish. Immigration has brought hundreds of different languages into the country. However, some American-English words are different. Have a look at the words below.

Words US	We say...
soccer	football
movie	film
chips	crisps
fries	chips
color	colour
airplane	aeroplane
gas	petrol
cookie	biscuit
fall	autumn
pants	trousers
vacation	holiday
faucet	tap
bathroom	toilet
cookout	barbeque
recess	break-time

My map of the USA

Trace this map, colour it in and use the map on page 5 to write the names of all the places.

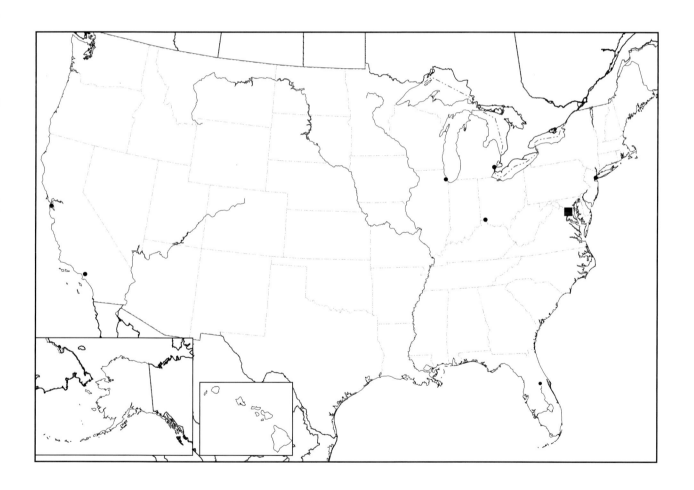

Index